CTS Prima

Religious Education

The Way, the Truth & the Life Series

Pupil Book

**Amette Ley
Ged Clapson
& Louise McKenna**

CATHOLIC TRUTH SOCIETY
PUBLISHERS TO THE HOLY SEE

Introduction

Welcome to *'The Way, the Truth & the Life'* series.

Think about the name of this series of books.

It is Jesus who said: "I am the Way, the Truth and the Life" *(Jn 14:6)*. These are very important words, so I would like each one of you to ask Jesus to help you to understand them.

In your lessons in religious education this year you will become familiar with the Bible: the story of God's love and concern for all of us. You will study the life of Jesus, and learn some of his important teachings. You will also learn that Jesus is our Saviour, and spend time learning about his death and resurrection.

You will study more about the seasons that the Church celebrates, especially the time of Holy Week and Easter. As you progress through this book, you will get to know about the birth of the Church and what it means to belong to it.

I hope you will enjoy your study and that each day you will grow closer to Jesus himself, who loves us and sends us his peace.

Vincent Nichols

✠ Vincent Nichols
Archbishop of Birmingham

Contents

1. The Bible

The Bible story

The Bible tells the story of God's relationship with his people, his concern for them and their response to his love.

The Bible is made up of many books. It was written over hundreds of years by many different writers. It starts with creation, the beginning of time, and covers the history of many people.

Each book in the Bible tells a section of the story of how God guides his people into the way of truth, goodness and love. Often people do not understand what God is telling them and some deliberately choose to go their own way. Others worship false gods, such as money, and there are those who cause great suffering to other people.

No matter how many leaders, kings and prophets God sent, the people did not really understand what God wanted. Therefore God sent his own son, JESUS, into the world to save everyone - all of us too.

The first forty-six books of the Bible record the history of God's people - his chosen people, the Israelites. This section is called the Old Testament. It begins with the book of Genesis and ends with the book of Malachi.

The New Testament is made up of the books about Jesus and the early Church. It begins with the Gospel of Matthew and ends with the book of Revelation.

These books record the life and teachings of Jesus. They tell us where he was born, how he lived and died to save us and how God raised him to life again. Some of the books tell us about his followers, the early Christians. They explain how they set out to tell everyone they met about Jesus and how the Church began.

The books of the Old and New Testament were put together to form the Bible.

 ## Activities

1. Bible Facts

    (a) What are the two main sections of the Bible?
    (b) What is the Old Testament about?
    (c) What is the New Testament about?

2. How would you explain what the Bible is to someone who is not a Christian?

3. Design a cover for a Bible that will give others an idea of what it is about. You can add information for the back cover if you wish.

4. Make a list of any stories from the Bible that you already know, then answer the following:

    (a) Which is your favourite story in the Bible?
    (b) Why do you like it?
    (c) What is its message for us today?

5. In groups, share your favourite stories and choose one to share with the class.

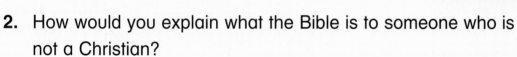

Word Box
New Testament
prophets
false gods   worship
Old Testament

In the beginning...

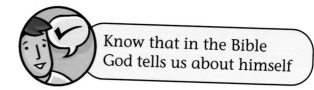

Before anything existed, before the world and everything in it were created, even before there was time, God already existed as God the Father, God the Son, and God the Holy Spirit, not three Gods - but three persons in one God. We call this the Holy Trinity.

God was filled with love that he wanted to share, so he created the heavens and the earth.

God said, "Let there be light" and there was light. Every time God spoke, he created something new. Pause for a moment and think of all the things he created: sun, moon, sky, oceans, mountains, trees, flowers, birds, animals.

Then God created men and women to enjoy all the wonderful things in the world and to know, love and serve him. He wanted them to be his friends. He called them Adam and Eve. They were given everything they needed. God loved them and promised to take care of them.

He told them not to eat the fruit of 'the tree of good and evil'. If they obeyed God, they would be happy forever. However, Adam and Eve listened to another voice, and they disobeyed God. They chose to do what they wanted. Their disobedience brought selfishness and suffering into the world, not only for themselves, but also for their descendants, that is, their children and their children's children and all people.

When God inspired people to write the story of his relationship with us, he wanted to explain what he is really like. When we read the Bible, we start to understand who God is.

Activities

1. Some of the following sentences are **true** and some are **false**. Correct the ones that are **false** and re-write them in your book.

   (a) God created the world.

   (b) God forgot to create animals.

   (c) Adam and Eve always obeyed God.

   (d) God wants us to love and serve him.

2. **(a)** Think about the part of Creation you would miss most if it disappeared.

   (b) Write what it is and why you would miss it.

   (c) Write a short 'thank you' prayer for that part of Creation.

3. Imagine God asks you to tell him what you are like.

   (a) Make a list of some of the things you would tell him.

   (b) What do you think he would say about your list?

4. God existed before time began and will always exist in the future. He has no beginning and no end. A circle is sometimes used to remind Christians of this.

   (a) Draw a circle and add a caption that explains why it is used as a symbol of God.

   (b) List some ordinary things that are circular that would be a good way of reminding Christians about God.

   (c) Explain why you chose them.

> ### Word Box
> Holy Trinity   disobedience
>   create

Abraham and Moses

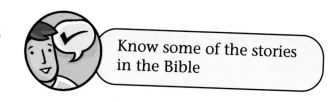

Through Abraham, God shows his people that if they have great faith and complete trust in him he will look after them.

God chose an old man, Abraham, and asked him to leave the place where he was and go to a land that he would show him.

Abraham said yes to God, even though that meant leaving everything he knew.

He took his belongings and set off with his wife Sarah. He did not know where he was going.

God promised Abraham and Sarah that they would have a son and a land of their very own.
He even said that the number of their descendants would be more than the stars in the sky or the sand on the seashore.

Can you imagine what great faith they must have had to believe all this, especially as they were both very old! But God always keeps his promises and after many years, his promise came true.

Through Moses, God shows his people that he is all-powerful and will look after them.

God chose Moses to lead his people out of slavery in Egypt. Moses was terrified by God's command. He didn't think he would be able to speak to the great king, Pharaoh of Egypt, and convince him to free God's chosen people.

Moses had to learn to listen to the voice of God and to trust in him. By doing so, he saw some amazing events. He even saw the Red Sea divide to let God's chosen people, the Israelites, go through. Then it closed in on their enemies, the Egyptians, and they were drowned.

Every year the Jewish people remember and celebrate the story of how they escaped from Egypt.

Activities

1. Why do you think Abraham left everything and started out on a journey?

2. How do you think Sarah felt when Abraham told her that they would be leaving to go on a very long journey?

   Draw a heart and inside it write what you think Sarah might have felt.

3. What would you miss the most if you had to move and leave almost everything behind?

4. Your teacher will give you the story about Moses and the Exodus. Read it carefully. Describe how Moses convinced Pharaoh that he had to let the Israelites go free. You could choose a part from it to make into a short play.

David

Through David, God shows his people that if they trust in him, he will give them courage and strength to overcome difficulties.

Even though the Israelites saw the power of God in many ways, they began to grumble. They wanted a king like other nations. In time, God chose a young boy, David, to be their king. Just then the people were at war with the Philistines who had a very powerful army. Their leader was a huge warrior called Goliath - almost a giant! The Israelites were terrified of him. Soon, David who was young and small let them know that he had a giant of a God with him - he knew that with God's help he could do anything that God wanted.

You will have to find out what happened when he went to meet the giant Goliath with only his sling in his hands.

Activities

1. Either read or listen to the story of David and Goliath.

2. Which section of David's story did you enjoy the most?

3. Why do you think this story should be included in a book of Bible Stories for young children?

4. Imagine David is telling his grandchildren about what happened to him and Goliath

   (a) What would he want them to learn from his story?

   (b) What could people today learn from his story?

Word Box

warrior

descendants   Philistines

Jonah

This story shows how God cares enough not to let people carry on doing wrong, hurting themselves and others.

You would think that when people saw how powerful God could be that they would go on their knees and worship him. Some did for a little while, but they soon grew tired and impatient. They didn't care about the poor, the sick and the lonely. They only thought about having lots of good things for themselves.

God knew his people would never find happiness like that. He wanted them to repent and live good lives. He didn't want them to be unhappy and he didn't want to punish them. So God sent many prophets to warn them about the wicked lives they were living.

Jonah was one of the prophets God chose. He told him to go to Nineveh to warn the people to change their ways. But Jonah disobeyed God. He didn't care if the people were punished. He was afraid they might kill him if he went there so he sailed off in the opposite direction. God was angry with Jonah. A great storm arose at sea and an enormous fish swallowed him. Jonah repented and prayed to God. God heard his prayer and saved him. Then Jonah went to do God's work. You will have to read the whole story to find out the details.

 **Activities**

1. **(a)** Find out about the story of Jonah.

   (b) Draw Jonah's face when God called him. Add a caption to explain how he felt.

   (c) What lessons did Jonah have to learn?

   (d) How did God teach Jonah these lessons?

   (e) What can we learn from the life of Jonah?

   (f) What does the story tell us about God?

2. In groups, choose one of the following stories:

   (a) David and Goliath.

   (b) Moses and the Exodus.

   (c) Jonah.

3. **(a)** Write a scene for a play, telling what message the story has for today.

   (b) Practice the scene so that you can perform it for an audience.

   ___

   ## Word Box

   repented   Nineveh

Mary

Through Mary, God came down to earth and lived among his people.

Mary was a young girl who loved God very much.

When an angel appeared to her and asked her to be the mother of Jesus, the Son of God, she was amazed.

She trusted in God and said, 'yes', she would do whatever God wanted her to do. Because of this Mary is known everywhere.

She is sometimes called the Mother of God or Queen of Heaven. She is our mother too. In heaven, she asks God for many graces and blessings for us.

Activities

1. Write down two reasons why you think Mary is so important.

2. (a) Draw a picture of the angel appearing to Mary.

   (b) Describe how you think Mary felt on that day.

   (c) What do you think Mary asks God for when she prays for us?

3. Think about what you already know about Mary.

   Why do you think the message of the angel was one of the most important events in the whole world?

   You could present your answer as a speech, written or recorded.

Word Box

graces

blessings

angel

God speaks to us in the Bible

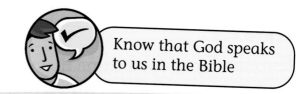

Sometimes the readings in the Bible sound great - they help us to understand things, they encourage us, they comfort us when we are afraid.

At other times they remind us to love others and that's not always easy. Some readings can be really difficult to take - like 'love your enemies!'

14

Activities

1. Slowly and quietly read the quotations on page 14.

   Read them a second time and think carefully about each one.

   (a) Which one makes you feel happy?

   (b) Make a copy of this one and decorate it, using colour to show the key words.

   (c) Write down underneath it why it makes you happy.

2. Look at the Bible references again.

   Which one will help a person...

   (a) who is worried about something;

   (b) to forgive when he/she has been hurt;

   (c) not to judge others;

   (d) to trust in God?

3. Read the quotations again.

   (a) Choose one that you find hard to do and write it down.

   (b) In silence, spend a few moments asking God to help you to live that message.

4. Look up the following references and write them out in your own words.

   Luke 6:27   John 14:14

   John 15:12   John 14:27

   Matthew 7:1   John 14:1

Finding a Bible reference

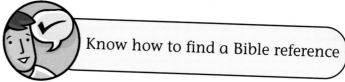

The Bible is a big book with many pages.

Do you know where you would find the passage below?

So he called a little child to him and set the child in front of them. Then he said, 'I tell you solemnly, unless you change and become like little children you will never enter the kingdom of Heaven.'

(Matt 18:2-3)

Look at the words in red underneath the passage: **Matt** which is short for Matthew, tells you in which 'book' you will find the quotation.

The first number, **18**, tells you which chapter of the book it is in and the numbers after the colon (:) tell you which verse or verses from that chapter.

So we have the Gospel of St Matthew, chapter eighteen, verses two to three.

Now open your Bible and see if you can find the passage.

First of all, go to the New Testament near the end of the Bible and find Matthew's Gospel.

That should be easy because it is the first book of the New Testament.

Now find chapter eighteen.

Look for the small numbers that mark the verses. Verse two begins, *'So he called a little child...'*

16

Activities

1. **(a)** What is the name of the first Book in the Old Testament?

    (b) What is the name of the first Book in the New Testament?

2. **(a)** Look up the following Bible references:

    > Luke 16:10

    > Mark 9:37

    > John 14:1

    (b) Write down what each person said.

    (c) Choose one reference and say when it might help someone to read this passage.

3. In the Old Testament we read of many promises God made to his people.

    Find one or two of the references below and write out the promise with the reference next to it.

    > Genesis 9:15

    > Isaiah 54:10

    > Isaiah 56:1

4. Would you find the following in the Old Testament or New Testament?

    The first one is done for you.

    (a) God created Heaven and Earth.

    Old Testament

    New Testament ☐

    (b) The story of Noah, the flood and the Ark.

    (c) The Angel Gabriel visits Mary.

    (d) The baby Moses is left among the bulrushes.

    (e) The book of Psalms.

    (f) The Gospel according to Mark.

    (g) The story of the baptism of Jesus.

2. Trust in God

Learning to Trust

Emma could not wait to get to the swimming pool. But last term, swimming filled her with fear. She was frightened of the water. But she had trusted the swimming instructor about learning to swim. Maybe trusting in God was just the same...

Jesus often taught his disciples how important it is to trust in God. Jesus sometimes had to remind his disciples to have faith and trust him.

Jesus calms the storm

One day, Jesus was in a boat with his disciples. They were on the Sea of Galilee, which is really a huge lake.

Jesus wants us to trust him completely. He loves us so much that he wants us for himself. He wants us to rely on him for everything and to keep our hearts free to love and to trust in him. He can then fill our hearts with love that we can share with others.

In order to make sure we do keep our he rts free for him, Jesus makes great promises to us: he tells us that we don't need to worry about our lives, or about what we are going to eat or the clothes we wear. He knows we need all these things, and asks us to trust God and not to fill our hearts with worry about them.

"Let's go across to the other side of the lake," Jesus said. So they set out, and as they sailed, Jesus fell asleep. Soon, the wind began to blow very hard, the waves got bigger and the boat began to fill with water. The disciples were afraid. They went and woke Jesus.

"Master," they said, "Wake up! The boat is going to sink and we will drown!"

Jesus woke up. "Quiet!" he told the wind and the waves, and at once the storm died down. Jesus looked at his disciples.

"Where is your faith?" he asked them. The disciples began to wonder who Jesus really was.

Even the wind and the water obeyed him.
(Matt 8:23-27)

 Activities

1. Imagine you are in the boat with Jesus and the boat begins to sink. What would you say to him that shows you trust him?

2. Look at these words. Pick out those that would help us to trust in God.

self control	a big house	generosity
goodness	toys truthfulness	money
clothes	kindness	justice
anxiety	a bigger car	gentleness

3. (a) Spend a few minutes thinking about Jesus calming the storm.

   (b) What lesson did Jesus want to teach the disciples who were with him?

   (c) What do you think we can learn from this miracle?

Trusting is not always easy

Sometimes it can be very hard to trust, to really be sure that everything is going to be all right. Read what happened to Tom:

The children were watching TV. "What's all that noise about outside?" Abigail asked. "I can smell burning!" said Tom, and they rushed to the window.

Outside there was a crowd of people shouting and pointing up at their flat! Flames and a big cloud of smoke were coming from their block.

"There's a fire engine!" Rebecca shouted. Tom looked out too. "It's the fire brigade!" he said. "They're coming to rescue us!"

There were firemen below, setting up a huge trampoline for the children to jump to safety. "Jump !" shouted one of the men, "We'll catch you."

Rebecca climbed on the windowsill and took a deep breath.

She shut her eyes and jumped, landing safely on the trampoline.

Then Abigail jumped as well. Now it was Tom's turn. He looked down. He couldn't see where he would land if he jumped. He felt his legs begin to shake.

"I don't think I can do this," he called. "I'm afraid." "Come on, lad," shouted one of the firemen, "We'll catch you."

"Don't be afraid, Tom," called Abigail "You'll be quite safe. The trampoline is strong and made just for this - you can trust it."

Tom felt very shaky, but he knew he had to trust. "OK," he said, shut his eyes, and jumped. Strong arms reached out to catch him - he had made it! "It was difficult to trust, but I'm glad I did", he thought.

Activities

1. There are many things that help us to trust in God.

   (a) Look through the following list.

   > Receiving Jesus in Holy Communion
   >
   > Going for a walk
   >
   > Talking about God with other people
   >
   > Trying to live by God's rules
   >
   > Listening to music
   >
   > Praying to God
   >
   > Something else that you can think of...
   >
   > Asking the saints and angels to pray for you
   >
   > Talking to a friend
   >
   > Reading about God in the Bible or a book of Bible stories
   >
   > Learning about God in school

   (b) Which of the above do you think will help you to have more faith and trust in God?
   Put them in the order you would find most helpful.

   (c) Choose one and write why you think this will help you.

2. **(a)** Write a letter encouraging an imaginary friend who is finding it hard to trust in God.

   or...

   (b) Write an answer to a letter in a magazine to someone who has written in saying how hard it is to trust in God at the moment.

3. Find out about one of these saints and write how he or she had to trust in God at a difficult time in his or her life.

   St Paul

   St Thomas a Becket

   St Francis of Assisi

   St Andrew

   St Bernadette

   St Stephen

   St Thérèse of Lisieux

The promise God made to Zechariah

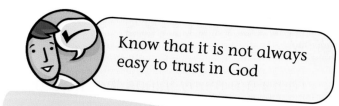

Sometimes we make a promise and it is too hard for us to keep. Sometimes, too, someone makes us a promise and we think, 'That's too good to be true!'

When God makes a promise, he always keeps it. He had promised to send a Saviour who would share his life with us. Now the time was right.

Zechariah was in the Temple in Jerusalem. He was a priest and he was offering prayers to God.

As he prayed, he looked up and saw an angel. It was the Angel Gabriel.

Zechariah was afraid, but the Angel Gabriel had good news for him.

'Your prayers have been heard, Zechariah,' he said. 'You and your wife Elizabeth are going to have a baby son.

You must call him John. He will bring you great happiness.

When he is grown up, he will help many people to love God.'

Zechariah felt very happy to hear this but wondered if it could be true.

He and Elizabeth had wanted a baby for so long and now they were going to have a child who would be the greatest of all the prophets! It was hard to believe such wonderful news.

'How do I know this is true?' he asked the angel.

'I was sent from God to tell you this,' the angel explained.

'As you did not believe me, you will not be able to speak until the baby is born.'

Everyone in the temple was very surprised when they realized that Zechariah could not speak to them.

Zechariah went home and waited.

When the time came for Elizabeth and Zechariah's baby to be born, all their family and neighbours wanted to name him Zechariah, after his father.

'No', said Elizabeth firmly, 'His name is John.'

'But nobody in your family has that name,' the people said.

They gave Zechariah a writing tablet where he could write the baby's name.

Zechariah wrote, 'His name is John.'

As soon as he had written this, he found he could speak again.

God had kept his promise to Zechariah and all the neighbours wondered who John would grow up to be. (Luke 1:5-24, and 57-66)

St John the Baptist

Activities

1. Zechariah could not speak for a very long time.

   He must have had to write down what happened so that his family knew.

   Imagine you are Zechariah.

   Write down what he might have written for his family when he came home from the Temple.

2. It is sometimes difficult for us to keep our promises.

   (a) Describe a time when you or someone you know made a difficult promise and kept it.

   (b) Write what made the promise difficult to keep.

3. In groups, make a prayer that asks for God's help to trust in him.

   Each person could think of a time when we specially need to trust God.

   You could begin like this:

   When we are lonely - help us to trust in you.

Activities

4. **(a)** Why do you think Zechariah didn't believe what the angel said?

Was it because:

He had never seen an angel before

He thought the news was too good to be true

He thought that both he and Elizabeth were too old to have babies

He didn't trust in God

Another reason

Choose one reason.

(b) Draw a picture of Zechariah with a 'thought bubble' and write the reason you have chosen inside it.

(c) Write a sentence to explain why you chose this reason.

5. Sometimes it is hard for us to trust that God knows what is best for us. Write about a time when you found it hard to trust in God and explain why it was difficult.

6. The angel brought a special promise from God about John.

(a) Look up **Luke 1:15**.

(b) What was the promise?

	Word Box	
prophets		writing tablet
anxiety	justice	Temple
		self-control

25

The promises God made to Mary

The Angel Gabriel was sent from God to a young girl named Mary.
The angel said:

**'Hail Mary, full of grace!
The Lord is with you.'** (Luke 1:28)

Mary was deeply disturbed by these words and asked herself what this
greeting could mean, but the angel said to her,

**'Mary, do not be afraid;
you have won God's favour.'**

The angel explained to Mary, that she would be the mother of a baby boy,
and she was to call him Jesus. He would be great and would be called the Son
of God. Mary was puzzled because she was not married. She asked the angel
how this would happen.

The angel explained that the Holy Spirit would come upon her, and her baby would be the Son of God.

Gabriel reminded Mary that nothing is too hard for God. He told Mary that her cousin Elizabeth, whom everyone thought was too old, was going to have a baby in three months time.

'I am the handmaid of the Lord,' Mary said. 'I will do what you have said.' This was Mary's way of saying 'Yes, I trust you,' to God. And the angel left.

God always keeps the promises he makes. Like Mary, we can learn to trust and have faith in God, because he loves us and wants us to be happy.

Activities

1. Look at the picture of Mary with the angel.

    (a) What do you think Mary is thinking?

    (b) Draw Mary with some 'thought bubbles'.

    (c) Write in them what you think Mary might
        be thinking as she listens to the angel.

2. Imagine an artist has been asked to paint a picture of this story.
    What would you need to tell him about the story to make sure he
    gets the picture right?

    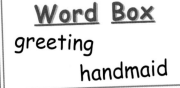

3. Mary and Zechariah were both puzzled by the messages of the angel.
    But we know that Mary trusted God more than Zechariah because of the
    angel's replies to them.

    (a) Look up **Luke 1:19-20** and **Luke 1:37**.

    (b) Write the angel's words to Mary and to Zechariah.

> **Word Box**
> greeting
>   handmaid

Joseph put his trust in God

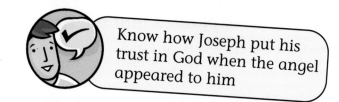

Know how Joseph put his trust in God when the angel appeared to him

Mary trusted God and agreed to be the Mother of Jesus. She trusted God to look after her.

Mary was engaged to a good and gentle man named Joseph.

Now Mary had to trust God to help Joseph understand that her son would be the Son of God. God knew the right time and the right way to speak to Joseph about this.

An angel came to Joseph in a dream and said:

"Joseph, son of David, do not be afraid to take Mary as your wife, for that which is conceived in her is of the Holy Spirit: she will bear a Son, and you shall call his name Jesus, for he will save his people from their sins." (Matt 1:20-21)

Mary was to be the mother of Jesus. Joseph was to be the foster father of Jesus. Joseph always obeyed and trusted God. He became a strong guardian for Mary and for Jesus.

After Jesus was born, Joseph had another dream. The angel warned him that King Herod wanted to harm Jesus. Joseph trusted God and he believed what the angel told him.

"Rise, take the child and his mother, and flee to Egypt, and remain there till I tell you, for Herod is about to search for the child, to destroy him." (Matt 2:13)

Joseph took Mary and Jesus all the way to Egypt. He trusted God to look after them and bring them safely home again. The Holy Family, Jesus, Mary and Joseph, lived in Egypt until it was safe for them to return home to Nazareth.

Activities

1. **(a)** Look at this list of things Mary had to trust God to do when she said 'yes' to him.

   Mary had to trust God -

   • to help Joseph understand that her baby was the Son of God;

   • to let the baby be born safely in the place God chose;

   • to protect her and the baby from all danger.

Escape to Egypt

   (b) Choose one, and explain why Mary might have been anxious.

   You could begin like this:

   "Mary might have been worried that..."

2. In what ways did Joseph have to trust in God?

   (a) Write down two of them.

   (b) Which one do you think was the most difficult? Explain why.

3. Look in **Matthew 1:21**. Why did the angel say Joseph must give Mary's son the name 'Jesus'?

4. **(a)** Which of these words do you think best describes Joseph?

   trusting   strong
   frightened
   disobedient
   caring
   hardworking
   selfish

   (b) Write a sentence which begins, 'I think Joseph was...'.

   ...or write the words in 'bubble letters' and decorate them to show their importance.

   (c) Write reasons for your answers.

God fulfils his promise

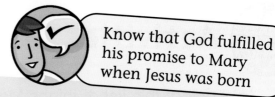
When it was almost time for Mary's baby to be born, Joseph and Mary had to go on a journey to a town called Bethlehem, King David's city.

This was a long way from their home in Nazareth.

The Roman Governor had ordered that everyone must travel to the town where their families first came from.

When they arrived in Bethlehem, it was very crowded.

Lots of people had travelled there and all the places to stay were full.

Mary knew her baby would soon be born.

Joseph was getting anxious and Mary was very tired so they just had to settle for an old stable with animals in it.

Mary's baby son was born that night and she wrapped him up and laid him in the manger, the animal's feeding-trough.

God had kept his promise to Mary. The Saviour of the world had come.

Mary kept all these things that happened in her heart.

She thought about them and remembered them.

Later on she told other people all that had happened.

 # Activities

1. The Angel Gabriel had told Mary that her Son would be great.

   (a) In what kind of a place do you think a great king would be born?

   (b) Draw a picture of it and label all the things a baby king might have.

   (c) Now draw another picture of the kind of place where Jesus was born and label the things he had.

2. (a) Think about the Nativity story.

   Choose a character, a time, a place and the weather.

   (b) Now write your account of what happened using the character you have chosen.

   For example, you could be a shepherd, at midnight, on the hills where it is very cold, or a donkey, waking up in the morning, in the stable with the sun shining on the snow.

3. What was the news that the angel brought to the shepherds?

   (a) How would they know it had come true? **(Clue - Luke 2:2-12)**

---

engaged

Word Box

foster father

Nazareth

guardian

Roman Governor

conceived

3. Jesus, the Teacher

Jesus was born a Jew

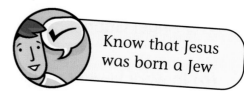

Know that Jesus was born a Jew

Jesus was born into a Jewish family. His parents, Mary and Joseph, were faithful Jews and always followed the Jewish religion and laws. When they went to the synagogue in Nazareth on the Sabbath day they took Jesus with them.

At the synagogue there are prayers and hymns. The people say together the Shema - a statement of what the Jewish people believe about God.

> 'Listen, O Israel:
> The Lord our God is one.
> Love the Lord your God with all your heart and with all your soul and with all your strength.'

Then the scrolls with the Word of God written on them are brought out from the Ark. These scrolls, known as the Torah, contain the first five books of what Christians now call the Old Testament.

Everyone listens while the word of God is read. After this, a Rabbi, or teacher, is asked to talk about the readings. At the end of the service there is a blessing.

Activities

1. Make a 'passport' for the young Jesus. Use the following headings to help you:

   - Nationality:
   - Parents:
   - Religion:
   - Place of birth:
   - Town:

   You can include a picture if you wish, and any other information you can think of.

2. Look up **Deuteronomy 5:12** in the Bible. In your own words explain what God asks the Jewish people to do on the Sabbath.

3. The **Shema** is a statement of what the Jewish people believe about God. It is found in the Old Testament. You'll find the first part on page 32.

   Look up **Deuteronomy 6:4-9** and write down what God asked his people to do to help them remember these words.

4. Why do you think the words of the Shema are so important that the Jewish people repeat them every day?

5. Is there a prayer that is so important to you that you repeat it daily?

   (a) What is it?

   (b) Why is it important?

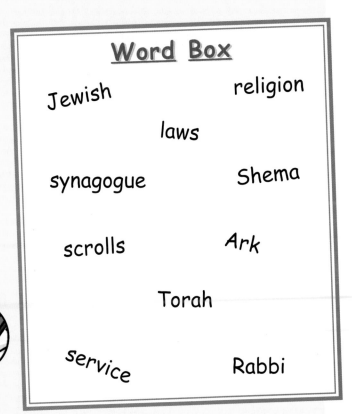

Word Box

Jewish   religion

                laws

synagogue   Shema

   scrolls   Ark

           Torah

service   Rabbi

The presentation of Jesus in the Temple

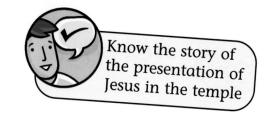

Know the story of the presentation of Jesus in the temple

Forty days after the birth of Jesus, Mary and Joseph travelled to the Temple in Jerusalem. As faithful Jews, they wanted to follow the Jewish law that said the first-born son in every family should be presented to God.

On that day Jesus was like a new 'light' coming into the world.

There was an old man in Jerusalem, called Simeon.

He was very close to God. God had made him a promise - he would not die before he had seen the Messiah, the Chosen One, sent by God to be a Saviour to His people.

As Simeon prayed in the Temple one day, a man and a woman came in carrying a small baby. Many people were coming in and out of the Temple, but Simeon knew who they were - Mary and Joseph with their son, Jesus.

Simeon took the baby Jesus into his arms and praised God for him.

He knew that Jesus would grow up to be the Messiah they had all longed for.

This is the prayer he said:

Lord, now let your servant depart in peace according to your word; for my eyes have seen your salvation which you have prepared in the sight of all the peoples, a light for the nations and the glory of your people Israel. (Luke 2:29-32)

God had kept his promise! He had sent the Messiah, and Simeon had seen him.

We remember this event in the life of Jesus on 2 February each year, at the feast called 'The Presentation of the Lord.'

Activities

1. Match these sentences with the people who might have said or thought them:

Joseph **Simeon** **Mary**

(a) "This is the Messiah - at last I have seen him."

(b) "We have come to present my child to God."

(c) "This old man is saying amazing things about Jesus."

2. Imagine you are a newspaper reporter and you were there in the Temple when Mary and Joseph brought in the child Jesus.

(a) Think of a headline for a report of what you saw and heard.

(b) Write the headline in large capital letters.

(c) Underneath, write a short report of the event, explaining what happened and why.

Word Box
presented

salvation

chosen one

Messiah

glory

Jesus, travelling and teaching

Jesus had been given a special mission. When he grew up, he spent a lot of his time teaching. He was a Rabbi, or teacher. He travelled around Galilee, sometimes teaching in synagogues and sometimes teaching outside, on a mountain or beside a lake. The Bible tells us that huge crowds gathered to hear Jesus, sometimes as many as four or five thousand people! Everyone listened to his wonderful teaching. At last, he returned to Nazareth where he had been brought up. When the Sabbath day came, he went into the synagogue as he always did.

When it was time for the readings, the scroll was handed to Jesus. He read from the book of the prophet Isaiah. Then, because he was a Rabbi, he sat down to teach the people what it meant.

The prophet Isaiah wrote about the Messiah who was coming to give the good news to the poor. Jesus explained to the people that he was making the words come true that very day.

Jesus' teaching

This is the Good News that Jesus brought: **God loves us so much that he sent his son, Jesus, to open the way to heaven for everyone.**

What was so important about what Jesus had to say to the crowds?

Why did his teaching leave them 'astonished' or 'amazed' as the Bible tells us it did?

A lot of what Jesus had to say was not new.

Jesus was a Jew and he reminded the Jewish people of what they already knew about God.

He reminded them of the Shema and how they should love God and keep his commandments. But he also had something new to teach them: he was bringing them good news.

Jesus taught the people that, if they believed in him and followed his teaching, they would one day live with him forever.

 Activities

1. **(a)** What is the Good News?

   (b) Why do you think that the Good News is so important?

2. Find **Luke 4:18** - fill in the good things that will come to these people when the Messiah comes:

The poor	They will hear the good news
The captives (prisoners)	
The blind	
The oppressed (Look up the word)	

Word Box
mission
commandments
Galilee

3. Who do you think are 'the poor' today? How can we help them?

Jesus came to show us the way to live

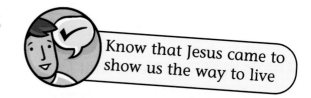

Jesus came to earth to teach us how to love and to help each other. In the way he lived, Jesus showed us how we should live as children of God. He knew that there is sin and hatred in the world. So he lived his life in a way that was full of love and goodness. He explained how we could all find happiness and peace, even though we may have difficulties and problems.

"Love your enemies and pray for those who persecute you." (Matt 5:44)

"Love one another as I have loved you." (John 15:12)

Jesus explains to us that when we help others, we please him very much. He said that whatever we do to others, to people we don't know, or people we think are not important, we do to him. He explains this teaching and says that the time will come when he will say to people who help others:

"Come, you that are blessed by my Father! I was hungry and you fed me, thirsty and you gave me a drink; I was a stranger and you received me in your homes, naked and you clothed me; I was sick and you took care of me, in prison and you visited me." (Matt 25:34-37)

The ones who truly followed Jesus will then answer him:

"When Lord, did we ever see you hungry and feed you, or thirsty and give you a drink? When did we ever see you a stranger and welcome you in our homes, naked and clothe you?

When did we ever see you sick or in prison, and visit you?

Jesus will reply, 'I tell you, whenever you did this for one of the least important of these brothers of mine, you did it for me!' (Matt 25:37-41)

Activities

Think about the following people:

Sick people

Refugees

Cold & Homeless People

1. **(a)** What is Jesus asking us to do about these people?

   (b) Why is it important that we follow his teaching?

2. **(a)** Make a list of six types of people Jesus asks us to help.

   (b) In pairs, choose one of these groups and suggest how you could help them.

   (c) Present your ideas to the rest of the class with illustrations.

3. Explain how the good things that you and other pupils will do to help others will make a difference to the lives of many people. You could present this as a flow diagram.

4. Write a list of 'good resolutions' that would help your class to be amongst the true followers of Jesus.

Jesus used parables to teach people

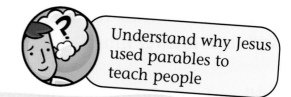

Jesus often told stories when he was teaching people. We call these stories parables.

A parable is an earthly story with a heavenly meaning.

Why did Jesus use parables to teach people?

He knew that the crowds enjoyed listening to stories especially those that were about things the people knew about, like sheep and vineyards, money, possessions and sowing seeds.

He knew that they were more likely to remember things they were told in this way - stories are much easier to remember than teaching!

He sometimes told them stories that would make them think - sometimes the story had something strange or unusual about it, which made the people think even harder.

Some parables were easier to understand than others. Sometimes Jesus told parables that not everyone understood. Even Jesus' disciples needed some of the parables explained to them!

Activities

The Parable of the Sower

1. **(a)** Read the Parable of the Sower from the sheet your teacher will give you.
   (Luke 8:4-8)

   (b) What happened to the seeds? Present your answers like the table below.

The soil where the seeds fell	What happened to them
On the path	
On the rocky places	
In with the thorns	
On good soil	

2. At the bottom of the page are the meanings Jesus gave to his disciples for the Parable of the Sower, but they are jumbled up.

   (a) Read the meaning of the parable for yourself in the Bible (Luke 8:9-15).

   (b) Write down each description of where the seeds fell and its correct meaning.

(i) those that fell by the path

(iii) those that fell among thorns

(ii) those that fell on rocky places

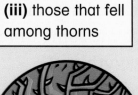

(iv) those that fell in good soil

Meaning: Those who do not understand the message of God because other things have stopped them.

Meaning: Those who hear the message of God but give it up when trouble comes.

Meaning: Those that hear the message of God, understand it and live by it.

Meaning: Those that hear the message of God but are worried by other things and ignore it.

41

Parables of Jesus

Why did Jesus teach in parables when they were sometimes hard for people to understand? The message he was giving them was a new message – the Good News – and the people needed time to get used to it.

So Jesus 'hid' the message in a story for them. Later on, they would understand the message of the story as well! Here is another parable Jesus told.

The Unforgiving Servant (Matt 18:23-35)

Once there was a king who decided to sort out the money people owed him. When he began to work out who owed what, one of his servants was brought to him. This servant owed the king a large amount of money. He could not pay the king back, so the king gave orders that he was to be sold, with his wife and his children and all that he owned. Then the king would get his money back.

The servant was really upset. He knelt down before the king and said, "Please, just give me some time and I will pay you everything I owe." The king felt very sorry for him, and said he would let him off the debt. The servant was very glad to hear this, and he left the room.

As he went out, he met one of his fellow servants who owed him a little money. "Pay me what you owe at once," he shouted, grabbing him by the throat.

The other servant knelt down in front of him. "Please, just give me some time and I will pay you everything I owe," he said. But the first servant refused and had his fellow servant put in prison until he could pay.

When all the other servants saw what had happened, they were very sad. They went to the king and told him all about it. The king was angry. He sent for the first servant again. "You wicked servant!" he said. "I let you off all the money you owed me, just because you asked. You should have done the same for your fellow servant." And the king had him sent to prison until he could pay everything he owed.

Activities

1. Look at the parable of the Unforgiving Servant.

   (a) Who do you think is most like God in this parable?

   (b) Look up **Matthew 18:35** and write out what Jesus said about how we should treat each other.

2. Imagine you are going to make a film of the Unforgiving Servant. Design a video cover for your film. Write part of the story on the back so that people will want to find out more.

3. What do you think would have happened if the first servant had let the second servant off the money he owed? Write a different end to the parable story. What would Jesus have said to the people at the end of your story?

4. Jesus usually told parables using things people knew about. If he was telling parables today, he might tell them differently. Tell the story of the Unforgiving Servant as if it happened today. You could present it as a storyboard or a TV script.

5. Design a wall poster to illustrate your favourite parable. Make sure the main characters are bold and clear and that the message is obvious.

4. Jesus, the Saviour

Jesus was truly human

Know that Jesus is truly God and, as man, truly human

When Jesus was born, he was a tiny baby just like any newborn baby. He grew up and went to a Jewish school, he had to study and he played with the other pupils.

When Jesus got older, he liked having good friends like Martha and Mary and their brother Lazarus. When he heard that Lazarus had died, he wept. He liked celebrating with people and went to weddings. Many people thought he was a great person. He made lots of friends particularly among sinners, the poor, the sick and beggars. He even visited their homes and had meals with them.

People were attracted to him and enjoyed listening to him, though at times he really made them think. Occasionally, he made some people feel uncomfortable, particularly if they were rich and did not share with others, for example, he said:

"It is easier for a camel to pass through the eye of a needle than for a rich man to enter the kingdom of God". (Luke 18:29)

Another time, he got really angry when he found people selling their goods in the Temple. He drove them out saying:

"My house will be a house of prayer. But you have turned it into a robbers' den". (Luke 19:45-46)

Jesus is truly God

As a man Jesus is truly human, but he is also truly God.

> "**God loved the world so much that he gave his only Son, so that everyone who believes in him may not be lost but may have eternal life.**" (John 3:16)

God sent his Son, Jesus, into the world to save us and give us eternal life.

The disciples had difficulty understanding this, but when they saw Jesus work miracles they knew he was no ordinary person.

They saw him cure the paralysed man, calm a storm at sea and they had even seen him walk on the waters.

Jesus not only did many extraordinary things, but he said many things to show that he was speaking the words of God.

He was the 'Word of God'.

He spoke with very great authority: he told us we had to love our enemies, do good to those who hate us and pray for those who persecute us.

He showed us how to do this on the cross.

It is certainly not easy to love our enemies or to do good to those who hate us, but with Jesus' help it is possible.

We believe Jesus is truly God and as a man truly human, and this is part of our faith.

 # Activities

1. (a) Draw three faces; one happy, one tearful and one angry face:

(b) Think about times when you felt like this.

(c) Write about a time when Jesus felt like this. Jesus wept when...

2. As a boy or a man, Jesus is truly God, but he is also truly human.

Think of all the things you already know about him.

Draw two boxes, in one give reasons to show why you think that Jesus is human and in the other that he is God.

I know Jesus is truly human, because...	I know Jesus is truly God, because...

For clues look back over what you have been studying this term and look up the following scripture references:

Mark 1:40-42

Mark 3:1-6

Mark 1:32

Luke 8:22-24

John 11:25

Mark 6:45-52

3. We believe Jesus is truly God and, as a man, truly human

In order to remember this mystery about Jesus, copy and highlight it in your own book.

4. Jesus was truly human.
Sometimes he got angry over things that were wrong, like the time when he chased those who were selling and buying in the Temple.

(a) Read what happened in **Luke 11:15-18.**

Can you think of times when you (or other people) get angry?

(b) Make two headings:

> Wrong to be Angry

> Right to be Angry

(c) List some of those times under the best heading.

(d) Try to explain why it was right or wrong to be angry for one of those times.

5. Jesus is truly God.
Sometimes he said and did things that only God could do.

(a) Read the story of how Jesus healed Jairus' daughter in **Luke 8:40-56.**

(b) Imagine you were in the crowd that day. Draw a picture of what it was like. Underneath the picture write what you thought about Jesus afterwards.

Word Box

Word of God   authority

Mass

eternal life   persecute

Sharing in the life of Jesus

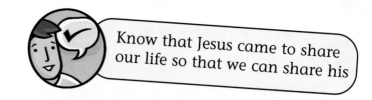

Know that Jesus came to share our life so that we can share his

Jesus has given us many ways of sharing in his life.
When we receive Holy Communion at Mass, we receive Jesus.
He is present in us in a very real way and will help us if we ask him.

> "He who eats my flesh and drinks my blood abides in me and I in him." (John 6:56)

If we believe and trust in Jesus, he will be with us and give us courage to overcome difficulties.

If we fail, he is always ready to forgive us if we ask him. We can receive the Sacrament of Reconciliation. This is when Jesus not only forgives us our sins, but he gives us the help we need to lead a good life.

When we pray, we grow close to Jesus.

He has told us that if we are worried or anxious about something, we can trust in him:

> "Do not let your hearts be troubled. Trust in God still, and trust in me." (John 14:1)

One day we will all die and leave this life on earth.

If we believe and trust in Jesus, he will give us true happiness now and eternal life with him in heaven forever.

> "I am the resurrection. If anyone believes in me, even though he dies he will live." (John 11:25)

Activities

1. Complete a sentence for each of the pictures.

Begin with the words:

(a) We share in the life of Jesus when...

(b) We share in the life of Jesus when...

(c) We share in the life of Jesus when...

2. Can you think of some other ways in which we share in the life of Jesus?

3. These sayings about Jesus are not true. Try to correct them.

(a) Jesus is only human.

(b) Jesus tells us to fight those who persecute us.

(c) Jesus tells us only to love those who are good to us.

(d) Jesus tells us not to give food to a hungry person.

4. When you have corrected the sentences above, choose one of them and describe how you put it into practice.

Word Box

abide

resurrection

reconciliation

sacrament

49

Jesus dies to take away our sins

We all know that the world is not always a good or happy place. There are many evil things happening in it: people being killed and hurt. There are people who are greedy and selfish, they cause a lot of pain where we would prefer to see love and joy.

When we know that something is wrong, but deliberately choose to do it, that is a sin. For example,

Jane knew that Paul had left a £5 note in his bag in the classroom. She watched him go out to the playground. No one was around, so Jane quickly put the money into her pocket.

Mike and John were playing football when one of them kicked it into one of the school windows and broke it.

Both boys decided not to own up to the head teacher.

In these situations Jane, Mike and John have committed sin.

They knew their actions were wrong, but chose to do what was evil.

There are times when we all know that we ought to do what is right, but choose to do what is wrong. When this happens it is a sin.

Jesus knew that he had to show us, not only how to lead a good life, but that he loves us so much that he is prepared to die to save us from our sins.

Mike's older brother Steve decided to take the blame for the broken window, so that Mike and John would not get into trouble.

In Old Testament times, God's people used to bring an offering or sacrifice, such as a lamb, to the Temple in Jerusalem to show God they were sorry and to try to make things right between themselves and God.

When Jesus died on the cross he was doing the same thing.

We call him the 'Lamb of God' because he was offering himself to God for all the wrong things people had done in the past or would do in the future.

Even though Jesus had never committed a sin he took the punishment for all our sins, on the Cross, a bit like Steve who took the blame for Mike and John.

Activities

1. You are at Mass, when it is over, imagine someone asks you to explain why the priest said:

   "Lamb of God, you take away the sins of the world: have mercy on us".

   What would you say?

2. Find illustrations of good and wrong actions.

   You can draw them, or cut out pictures.

   Create a classroom display with the bad things on the left, and the good things on the right - divided by a picture of Jesus on the cross.

3. Make a poster for display to remind everybody why Jesus came. Put in a reminder of what they need to do to thank him.

4. **"Oh my God, because you are so good, I am very sorry that I have sinned against you, and with the help of your grace, I will try not to sin again."**

   (a) Put a copy of this act of contrition into your book so that you can learn it.

   (b) Colour the key words to help you remember them, for example, God, good...

Word Box	
contrition	commit sin
sacrifice	Lamb of God

Palm Sunday

Do you know what happens when famous people arrive in a town after some great achievements, like winning a gold medal at the Olympics? Everybody comes out to greet them as they tour the town in an open bus, flags are flying and there is great excitement.

The people of Jerusalem greeted Jesus in much the same way nearly 2,000 years ago. Instead of a bus, he arrived on a young donkey. But the reaction of the crowd was much the same. They waved and cheered, because he was their hero.

They waved branches from the palm trees along the side of the road and laid their cloaks in front of Jesus like a carpet. That is why this day is called 'Palm Sunday'.

Some believed that he had arrived at Jerusalem ready to declare himself their king.

They thought he would lead a revolution against the Romans so that they would be able to rule themselves again.

But Jesus knew that he was going to Jerusalem for a very different reason.

The people all shouted at the top of their voices: "Hosanna! Hurray!

Welcome to you, Jesus! May God bless you! We want you to be a king like King David - we know you're descended from him. Hosanna! Hurray!"

"**Many people spread their cloaks on the road, others greenery which they had cut in the fields... all shouting, 'Hosanna! Blessings on him who comes in the name of the Lord!' "** (Mark 11:9-10)

Activities

1. Draw pictures to illustrate the following and put in 'speech bubbles' to show what they were either thinking or saying:

Jesus

the religious leaders

the crowds

Word Box

Romans   revolution

2. If Jesus entered your town today, what sort of welcome would you organize?

   (a) Make a plan to show what you would do.
   Think about the following:

   • What would you do to let people know he was coming?

   • Who would you invite to greet him first?

   • Who would you take him to see?

   • What kind of a celebration would you have?

   (b) Imagine you are the person to welcome Jesus. Write out what you would say.

   (c) What do you think Jesus would want to say to the people in your town?

Holy Thursday

The night before he died, Jesus wanted to share a Passover meal with his disciples.

They met together in an upstairs room and "as they were eating, Jesus took some bread, and when he said the blessing he broke it and gave it to the disciples.

'Take it and eat', he said **'this is my body.'**

Then he took a cup, and when he had given thanks he gave it to them.

'Drink all of you from this,' he said 'for this is my blood, the blood of the covenant, which is to be poured out for many for the forgiveness of sins.'" (Matthew 26:26-28)

On this night, Jesus gave his disciples the power to change the bread and wine into his body and blood.

This very great gift of Jesus himself is given to us each time we go to Mass and receive Holy Communion.

Even though we still see bread and we still see wine - yet in faith, we believe 'This is Jesus' body, this is Jesus' blood.'

Gethsemane

Jesus had invited his disciples to share his last hours with him. After they had finished their Passover meal, they went out of the city as usual to the Mount of Olives.

Jesus knew that he was going to suffer and die. So he took the disciples who were his closest friends, Peter, James and John and asked them to stay awake with him and watch and pray.

Jesus moved a little way off and began to pray. He asked God to save him from all the things that were going to happen.

But Jesus knew that the most important thing was to do what his Father wanted him to do, so he said to God - **"let it be as you want, not as I want it"** (Mk 26:39)

After accepting what God had in store for him Jesus went back to his disciples. "Look," he said, "the one who's going to betray me is coming..."

Judas, one of the twelve, led the guards to the Garden of Gethsemane and handed Jesus over to them.

The events of Holy Thursday

Even Jesus found it difficult to do what God wanted, but he trusted that in the end God would look after him.

On that Thursday - the Thursday of Holy Week - several very important things happened.

Jesus shared his Last Supper with his friends and gave them the power to change the bread and wine into his body and blood.

He gave us Holy Communion when he said that the bread was his body and the wine was his blood.

Jesus prayed in the Garden of Gethsemane, asking God to spare him the pain and suffering that he knew lay ahead.

But he also accepted willingly what God wanted of him.

Judas led the guards to the garden where Jesus was praying, so that they could arrest him.

Jesus was taken in front of the Jewish leaders where they accused him of claiming to be God's Son.

Jesus before the High Priest

Activities

1. Work in pairs.

   Imagine one of you is a journalist sent by the BBC to report on what has happened in Jerusalem, the other takes the part of a disciple who was present with Jesus.

   (a) Journalist interviews John about what happened at the Last Supper.

   (b) Journalist interviews James about Gethsemane.

   (c) Both write a report for the BBC on one of the two interviews.

2. Make a Holy Week diary and fill it in as you learn what happens on each day.

3. Complete the Thursday section of your Holy Week diary.

DAY	WHAT HAPPENED	WHERE CAN I FIND THIS IN THE BIBLE
Palm Sunday	Jesus rides into...	**Mark 11:1-11**

Word Box

Holy Week   Garden of Gethsemane

Last Supper

Passover meal   covenant   Judas

Good Friday

The death of Jesus

Jesus must have felt very alone as Thursday night turned into Friday morning.

All his friends had run off; Judas had betrayed him and the Jewish leaders had decided that he was guilty.

They were afraid that he would make himself their king.

But Jesus told Pilate that he was not the kind of king Pilate had in mind. He said: **"My kingdom does not belong to this world"** (John 18:36)

Then they put a cross on his shoulders and led him to a place called Calvary, which is where criminals were executed.

There, they nailed him to the cross and left him to die.

Jesus prayed for the people who had done this, asking God the Father to forgive them.

On either side of him there were two thieves being executed. One called over to Jesus and asked him to forgive him - Jesus replied that he would take him to paradise that same day.

In the last moments of his agony, Jesus offered himself to God, his Father and died.

At that moment, there was an earthquake and the rocks split open.

Jesus has made the most perfect offering of himself to the Father, and because of this he made it possible for us to enjoy heaven forever.

That is why we call this day Good Friday.

His friends took his body down from the cross and carried it to a new tomb that had been carved out of the rocks.

They wrapped him up hurriedly because it was nearly evening.

Then they rolled a heavy stone in front of the tomb to make sure that no one would disturb it and went off.

 ## Activities

1. Imagine you are an artist and you have been given the job of painting a picture of Jesus on Good Friday.

   (a) Write down all the important things that you would want to show in your picture.

   (b) Which people would be in the picture? Why?

2. Why do we call the day Jesus was crucified 'Good Friday'?

3. Complete the Friday and Saturday sections of your Holy Week diary.

Word Box

betrayed   guilty   Calvary   paradise   executed   criminal

Easter Sunday

When Jesus' friends went to the tomb, his body was gone!
They found it hard to believe, but then they remembered that he had said this would happen:
"After three days, I will rise again".

He was alive again. He appeared to his closest friends - including Mary Magdalene, who had gone to the tomb early on Sunday morning.

"I arrived there just as the sun was rising and... I could hardly believe my eyes! The stone had been rolled away and the tomb was empty! Suddenly, I heard a voice behind me:

'Why are you looking in there for someone who's alive?'

I turned round and there was a man standing there - shining like an angel. 'Don't you remember what he told you: that he would be arrested and nailed to a cross? But then, after three days, he would rise from the dead?'

I was scared. I ran back to the room where the others were and told them what I'd found. I don't think they believed me, but Peter and John set off for the garden to see for themselves. They found it exactly as I'd told them: Jesus had gone. I stood outside the tomb, crying. Then someone was standing near me. I thought it was the gardener. 'Oh please,' I said to him. 'Can you help me? They've taken the body of my Lord away, and I don't know where they've laid him.'

Then I heard his voice: 'Mary!' he said. I suddenly realised that it was Jesus. He had risen from the dead, just as he'd said he would. I wanted to hold on to him, to never let him go.

Instead, he told me to run back to his friends and tell them he was truly alive!"

As Christians, we believe that the Resurrection of Jesus was the most important event in history. The Resurrection of Jesus proves that death is not the end, but that, if we believe in and trust in Jesus, we can overcome selfishness and fear.

Also it shows us that Jesus wants us to have happiness now and live forever with him in heaven. Every spring, we celebrate Easter Sunday, and recall how Jesus rose from the dead.

We also remember the events of Holy Week and how Jesus suffered and died. Every time we celebrate the Eucharist, the Mass, we live these events as well. As we say:

"Lord, by your cross and resurrection, you have set us free. You are the Saviour of the World!"

Activities

1. There are many people in the world who have not heard about the events of Holy Week.

   Work in groups, you can choose either to write a newspaper article or a radio broadcast to explain these events and their importance.

   Each group is to choose one of the following:

   - Palm Sunday
   - Holy Thursday
   - Good Friday
   - Easter Sunday

2. Make a poster to put in school or at home to announce the Resurrection of Jesus.

   Put in an explanation of what this means for all of us.

3. Complete your Holy Week diary by adding the events of Easter Sunday.

Word Box

Easter Sunday   tomb

Eucharist

5. Mission of the Church
Jesus appears to the disciples

After Jesus had risen from the dead, the disciples saw him and spoke with him several times.

One night, Peter said, "I am going fishing," and some of the other disciples said they would go with him. They got into the boat and fished all night long on the Sea of Galilee, but they didn't even catch one fish.

Just as day was breaking, Jesus was standing on the beach, but the disciples did not know who it was. Jesus called to them, "Have you any fish?"
"No," they called back.

"Put down the net on the right side of the boat," Jesus told them, "and then you will find some." So the disciples put down the net on the right side and they caught so many fish that the net was too heavy to pull in.

One of the disciples began to realise who it was and he said to Peter, "It is the Lord."

Straight away Peter put on his clothes, got out of the boat and jumped into the sea to go to Jesus.

The other disciples were left dragging the heavy net full of fish!

When they got to the beach, they saw a fire alight and some fish cooking on it, and some bread. "Bring some of the fish you have caught," Jesus said, "and come and have breakfast."

None of the disciples dared to say. "Who are you?" They knew it was the Lord.

(John 21:1-13)

Activities

1. Look up **John 21** and find out:

   (a) the names of two other disciples who went fishing with Peter **(John 21:2)**

   (b) the disciple who told Peter "It is the Lord" **(John 21:7)**

   (c) how many fish there were in the net **(John 21:11)**

2. Why do you think the disciples didn't recognise Jesus at first?

3. Imagine you were one of the disciples who was there when you met Jesus on the beach.

   Write an account of the fishing trip and breakfast. Put in your account the moment when you knew it was Jesus, and how you knew.

4. Work in pairs, make a picture of the important part of this story.

   Give your picture a title and put in some of the words or thoughts of the characters.

63

Jesus makes Peter head of the Church

When Jesus and the disciples had finished their breakfast by the Sea of Galilee, Jesus wanted to talk to Peter. He had an important mission for him. Jesus wanted Peter to be the leader of the disciples. The disciples had to be able to tell everyone the good news about Jesus: what he had taught them, how he died and rose again from the dead. But there was something to be sorted out first.

"Simon," said Jesus, using Peter's old name, "Do you love me?" "Yes, Lord," said Peter, "You know I love you."

"I want you to feed my lambs," said Jesus.

Jesus asked Peter this question three times. Each time Peter told Jesus that he did love him, and each time Jesus asked Peter to feed his sheep and lambs. Peter understood that Jesus wanted him to look after all those who would believe in him. He felt sad that Jesus had asked him three times about whether he loved him.

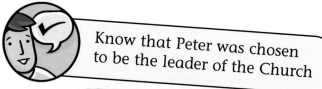

Know that Peter was chosen to be the leader of the Church

"You know everything, Lord," he said to Jesus. "You know I love you."

Perhaps Peter felt sorry, remembering that night when Jesus was arrested and taken to the High Priest's house.

That night Peter had denied three times that he even knew Jesus.

But Jesus gave Peter three chances to put that right when he asked if he loved him, and Peter knew he was forgiven. Jesus asked Peter to look after his Church.

Peter had to get ready to be the first leader of the Church on earth and it was not going to be an easy task.

Some time later, Jesus gave Peter and the other disciples their mission.

"Jesus said, 'All authority in heaven and on earth has been given to me. Go therefore, make disciples of all the nations: baptise them in the name of the Father and of the Son and of the Holy Spirit, and teach them to observe all the commands I gave you. And know that I am with you always; yes, to the end of time.' " (Mt 28:18-20)

Activities

1. **(a)** Why do you think Jesus trusted Peter again after he had let him down so badly?

   (b) What do you think Jesus said to Peter about it?

   (c) What do you think Peter said to Jesus?

2. **(a)** Make a list of the other disciples who were chosen by Jesus to help Peter spread the Good News.

   You can find their names in Luke 6:13-16.

   (b) What did Jesus do before he chose his disciples?
   (Luke 6:12)

3. **(a)** Read again the mission that Jesus gave to his disciples.

   (b) How do you know that they did what Jesus wanted them to do?

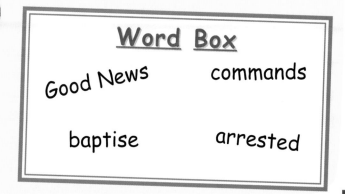

Word Box

Good News   commands

baptise   arrested

Jesus goes back to heaven

Know that the Church began at Pentecost

Jesus appeared to his disciples several times after he had risen from the dead.

He was preparing them to carry on his work.

"Stay in Jerusalem," said Jesus, "and wait for the Holy Spirit to come, as the Father promised.

Then you will receive power and you will be my witnesses all over the world."

One day, when he had finished talking to them, Jesus led them a little way out of the city; he lifted up his hands and blessed them and while they watched, he was taken up and a cloud took him out of their sight.

This event is known as the Ascension because Jesus ascended to heaven.

Every year we celebrate the feast of the Ascension of the Lord ten days before the feast of Pentecost.

The Ascension

The disciples and Mary, the mother of Jesus, returned to Jerusalem.

They were afraid and didn't know what to do next.

They locked themselves in the upper room talking about everything Jesus had said and wondered when the Holy Spirit would come.

The disciples wait for the Holy Spirit

One day as they prayed together the Holy Spirit came.

"Suddenly they heard what sounded like a powerful wind from heaven, the noise of which filled the entire house in which they were sitting; and something appeared to them that seemed like tongues of fire; these separated and came to rest on the head of each of them.

They were all filled with the Holy Spirit, and began to speak foreign languages as the Spirit gave them the gift of speech."
(Acts 2:1-4)

Suddenly, they knew that the Holy Spirit had come to them just as Jesus had promised.

They were immediately filled with new strength and courage.

All of them wanted to praise God and thank him for this gift.

Crowds of people came running to see what was going on.

Can you imagine their surprise when they heard the disciples speaking their own languages with the power of the Holy Spirit?

Peter stood with the eleven disciples and spoke to the crowd in a loud voice.

The Holy Spirit helped him as he told them the Good News.

Jesus is the Son of God.
He died and rose again.
He ascended into heaven.
He has sent the Holy Spirit today.

All the people were amazed.

"What shall we do?" they asked Peter. This was the message that Peter gave them:

"Repent and be baptised so your sins will be forgiven. You will receive the gift of the Holy Spirit. This promise is for you, and your children, and to all who are far away." (Acts 2:38-39)

That day, about three thousand people were baptised.

The Holy Spirit helped the disciples to teach them about Jesus.

Very quickly his teachings became known in different countries.

The Church had begun!

Peter Preaching

Activities

1. Work in groups: design a storyboard to illustrate the coming of the Holy Spirit at Pentecost using words and pictures

   Group 1 - Disciples huddled together in the upper Room.

   Group 2 - Holy Spirit comes down on the disciples.

   Group 3 - The disciples start speaking foreign languages.

   Group 4 - The disciples full of new courage greet the crowds.

   Group 5 - Peter gives the Good News to the crowds.

   Group 6 - Thousands of people are baptised.

2. Prepare for a quiz.

   When asked you must be able to complete these sentences.

   (a) Jesus told his disciples to wait in _____ until the Holy Spirit came.

   (b) Jesus was taken up into _____.

   (c) The disciples prayed with _____ while they waited for the Holy Spirit.

   (d) Lots of people were in Jerusalem for the feast of _____.

   (e) The Holy Spirit helped _____ speak to the crowd.

3. Create a glossary to give the meaning of the following words.

   Repent   Promise   Sins

   Forgive   Baptise   Power

   You may wish to use a computer.

Peter and Stephen

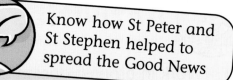

Soon even more people had been baptised and become part of the Church.
Now the disciples were called Apostles - Jesus had sent them on a mission - to do God's work. Peter was their leader - the first Pope.

Sick people were brought to the Apostles to be healed, just as they had been brought to Jesus. They came from all over the country. Sometimes the crowds were so great that sick people were laid down in the street so that at least Peter's shadow would pass over them in the hope that they would be healed.

Not everyone was so happy though. Before long Peter had been arrested and put in prison, but his work to spread the Good News was too important for him to stay there.

When the officers came to fetch him, they found all the doors locked and the guards standing outside - but there was no-one in the cell!
An angel of the Lord had set him free.

Many other people joined Peter and the Apostles to spread the news about Jesus. One of these was a young man called Stephen. Stephen had been chosen to help the apostles look after the people who needed food, and he wasn't afraid to say he believed in Jesus.

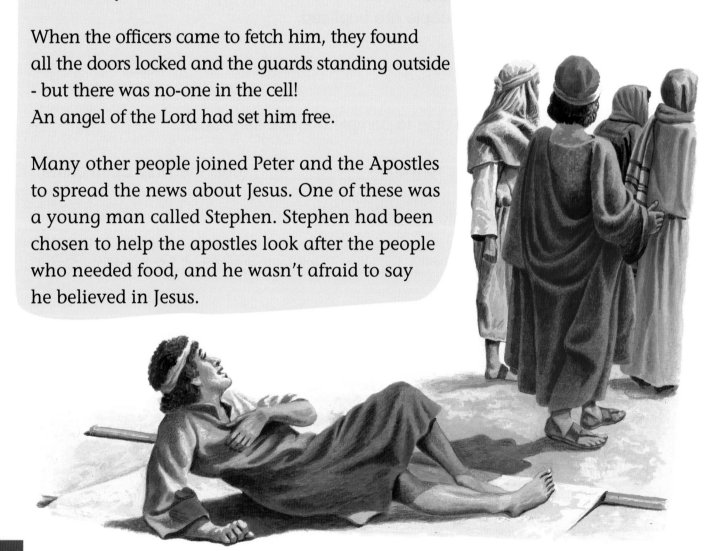

Soon Stephen was arrested too. When he spoke about Jesus, many people were angry. They took Stephen out of the city and stoned him to death. But Stephen could see Jesus in heaven and he forgave those who killed him. He was the first martyr of the Church.

Peter spent many years leading the Church. He went to Rome and guided the Church from there, but in the end, he too gave up his life for believing in Jesus. He is buried in Rome, underneath the church called St Peter's.

 # Activities

Quick Quiz

1. **(a)** What was the name of the first Pope?

   (b) What does the word Pope mean?

   (c) Who was the first martyr?

   (d) What does it mean to be a martyr?

2. We will probably not have to give up our lives because we believe in Jesus.

   Think about what you are prepared to give up because you believe in Jesus and follow him.

Look at this list:

- Give an hour on Sunday to go to Mass to be with Jesus.

- Spend ten minutes or so of playing time to pray to Jesus before going to bed.

- Give time to help your parents or tidy your things.

- Give some money to help poorer people.

   (a) Which of these do you find hardest to do?

   (b) Why do you think that is?

3. Write a prayer to St Stephen or St Peter asking them to pray for you and help you to be a stronger Christian.

Paul

As Stephen lay dying, a young man called Saul was watching. He agreed with Stephen's death. He didn't believe in Jesus at all and he was very angry with the people who did. Saul decided he had to stop the Church from growing any stronger. He was going to travel to a city called Damascus and hunt down any followers of Jesus he found there.

However, God had other plans for him. As he travelled to Damascus, something happened which would change his whole life, forever.

The Conversion of Saul

Suddenly, as he rode along, there was a bright light from heaven all round Saul. He fell to the ground. A voice was speaking to him.

"Saul, Saul, why are you persecuting me?" Saul was very puzzled. "Who are you, Lord," he asked. "I am Jesus," the voice replied, "and you are persecuting ME. Now get up and go into the city and you will be told what to do."

The men with him were standing around looking astonished. They heard the voice, but they couldn't see anyone.

For three days Saul was quite blind, until a Christian called Ananias prayed and gave him back his sight.

Soon Saul was baptised. Now he had a new name - Paul - and he went to see Peter. It was hard for the Apostles to believe Saul had really changed. Paul became one of the hardest workers in the Church. He made many long and dangerous journeys to tell people in other places about Jesus and his Church. He wrote many letters to the Christian communities in these places. At the end of his life, he too came to Rome and was put to death for teaching about Jesus.

Activities

1. Draw these spider diagrams into your book. On the end of each 'leg' write a word or phrase that describes the person in the middle. Here are some to help you get started: brave, angry, trying to destroy the Church.

2. Imagine you are Paul, going to see Peter and the Apostles for the first time.

(a) What do you think the Apostles would say when they saw you come into the room?

(b) What would be the first thing you would say to Peter?

(c) What would you offer to do to help spread the good news?

3. Match these sentence starters with the correct endings:

(a) Stephen died because…

(b) Saul wanted to stop people following Jesus because…

(c) Jesus spoke to Saul because…

(d) Saul was baptised because…

(e) The Apostles found it hard to believe Saul had changed because…

(f) Saul went on many long journeys to tell people about Jesus because…

…he told other people about Jesus.

…Jesus had really changed his life.

…he believed in Jesus now and wanted to join the Church.

…he wanted to kill Christians before he met Jesus.

…he wanted Saul to help him spread the good news.

…he didn't believe that Jesus had risen from the dead.

The Mission of the Church

Almost two thousand years have gone by since Peter, Paul and Stephen lived and died to tell people the good news that Jesus rose from the dead.
Now the Church that Jesus began is bigger than ever.

People all over the world have heard about Jesus. They have heard that he showed us how to live and that he died to save us, and that if we ask him, he will give us the strength to help each other. People from many countries have given up their lives to help to spread the Good News of Jesus.

However, there are still many people, even in our own country, who do not know the Good News. Everyone who belongs to the Church shares in the mission Jesus gave to his disciples.

The mission is to tell the whole world about Jesus and explain that they must love one another and to be ready to forgive each other when things go wrong. Everyone has his or her own way of doing this.

Some people are mothers and fathers and teach their children about Jesus.

Some people have a call from God to go out to another country, teach the people and show them how they should help each other.

Some are teachers in schools. They help pupils understand the life and teaching of Jesus.

Some people show the love of God through the way they do their work well, whatever work they do.

Some people have a call from God to become a priest, to be able to celebrate Mass and to give the sacraments to the people.

 # Activities

1. Find **Matthew 28:19-20** and write out the mission that Jesus gave his disciples after he had risen from the dead.

2. Think about how you can be part of the mission of the Church.

   (a) Who can you tell about Jesus?

   (b) What can you tell them?

   (c) What can you do to show love for others?

   (d) How can you live as Jesus asks?

   (e) Can you give an example of how Jesus has helped you or someone else?

3. Imagine you have to explain who Jesus is to someone who has never heard of him.

   Make an information leaflet about Jesus.

   Put in the most important things about him.

4. Design an invitation for someone to encourage them to come and be part of the Church.

   Think about the good things, but don't forget following Jesus can sometimes be difficult as well.

6. Belonging to the Church
First day at School

Know that you belong to a community

Can you remember your first day at a new school? How did you feel?

Excited?

A bit anxious?

You were arriving at a strange place, with lots of children and teachers you had not met before, everything looked so different.

How did you manage to find your way around the school, get to know the other children and find out the teacher's name?

Of course, everyone will have had different experiences on their first day at school. People made you feel welcome and helped you find your way around. Read Roger's description of his first day:

First day at School

A millionbillionwillion miles from home
Waiting for the bell to go. (To go where?)
Why are they all so big, other children?
So noisy? So much at home they
must have been born in uniform.
Lived all their lives in playgrounds.
Spent the years inventing games
that don't let me in. Games
that are rough, that swallow you up.

(Roger McGough)

 Activities

1. Write out the following statements about your class and fill in the gaps:

    There are ___ (number) members in this community.

    The leader of our community is _____.

    The purpose of our community is to _____.

    The main rule that we try to live by as a community is _____.

    The place where we meet is _____ .

2. Write down some words to describe how you felt on your first day at school.

3. Read the poem again.

    (a) Did Roger enjoy his first day at school?

    (b) Give four reasons for your answer.

4. In groups:

    (a) Think of some ideas that would make the school a happier place to be in.

    (b) Write them on a sheet of paper so that they can be put on the notice board.

- NOTICE BOARD -
Ideas for a happier school

Communities

We have another word for our school; we call it a **community**.

Each person in a community has a job. In the school community, teachers teach and pupils learn and make friends, and all the other staff help to make everything run smoothly.

Who made you feel welcome when you arrived at your school for the first time? Who explained what happens in your school? Did anyone tell you about the rules of the school?

You needed to find out about the different lessons, where the playground was, and what time the breaks were. Perhaps some of the older children helped you.

Did you make new friends that day? Now that you are older, can you help new children feel welcome when they join your school community?

Know that there are different types of communities

Some communities might have special features, like a uniform.

Communities usually have rules. Each member should keep these rules, but when someone breaks them, it can make things difficult for everyone in that community.

Every community has its **joys** - the good things that we get out of them, and its **challenges** - the things that the members have to do to make the community a success.

Being a member of a community means that we are mixing with people who share important things, or have similar ideas to us.
This can be fun and make life enjoyable. But it is also necessary for us to contribute (give) something to our community.

What other kinds of communities are there? Well, when we were born, we became a part of the human race.

We also belong to a family: parents, brothers and sisters, aunts and uncles, cousins and grandparents.

All of these are "communities". We were not able to choose whether to belong to the communities listed above - the human race and our families. That was decided for us when we were born.

Some people gather together in groups and make their own communities.

They support each other and usually have something that they all want to achieve - a purpose.

Activities

1. **(a)** Name a group or club to which you belong.

   (b) What activities do you do?

   (c) What rules do you have?

   (d) Do you have a badge or symbol for your group or club?

   (e) What do you enjoy most about being in your group?

2. Choose one community to which you belong.

   (a) Draw a large box in your exercise book and divide it into two columns with a line.

   (b) Put the name of the community you have chosen at the top of the page.

   (c) At the top of one column put **<u>Joys</u>** and the other **<u>Challenges</u>**.

   (d) Make a list of all the joys of belonging to the community.

   (e) Make a list of all the challenges you experience in the community.

3. Being a member of a community means that we need to do things in a certain way and obey the rules of that community.

   (a) Write down rules that are important for your school?

   (b) Explain why they are important.

   (c) Write down what things make a good community. Explain why.

The community of the Church

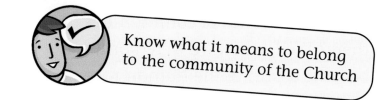

The Church is a community. It is the people of God who, for about 2000 years, have praised God and have tried to live holy lives as Jesus taught. This Church community has members all over the world… around 900 million of them! Members of the Catholic Church all have many important things 'in common', for example, they are all baptised. Beliefs that members of the Catholic Church share:

We believe that - Jesus is the Son of God, that he is the Saviour of the world and that he overcame death at the Resurrection. We also believe that he continues to be present in the Church today through the Holy Spirit.

We believe that - the Mass is the central event in the life of the Catholic Church and that Jesus is truly present when we receive him in Holy Communion.

We believe that - we are called to serve Jesus in the world today by spreading his message of love, joy and peace.

We believe that - the Pope is the successor of St Peter, the leader of the apostles. We believe that the authority that Jesus gave to Peter has been handed down to popes throughout the centuries.

There are also smaller Church communities.

A **Bishop** is the head of Catholics in a region known as a **diocese**.

Each diocese is divided up into **parishes**: these are small communities with a **church** where the people meet. A **priest** looks after the Catholics in his area and celebrates the Mass and the sacraments for them.

Activities

1. How can we serve Jesus?

   (a) At home?

   (b) At school?

2. In parish groups, prepare a presentation to show the rest of your class what happens in your parish.

   When you present it you can talk about it, using pictures and notices and anything else you can think of.

   TIPS

   • Be sure you know the name of your parish.

   • Be sure you know the name of your local priest.

   • Describe the activities for young people.

   • Describe who helps in the parish.

   • Name some celebrations.

   • Is there a Mass for young people?

3. Find out the name of the diocese that your school is in, and the name of the Bishop.

Word Box

beliefs   diocese   Bishop   parishes   priest

Becoming a Christian

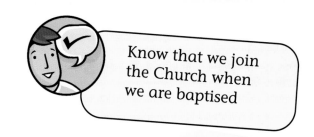

Know that we join the Church when we are baptised

When someone joins the community of the Church, there is a special celebration.

It is called **Baptism**, and it will often take place during Mass, so that all the other members of the community can welcome the new member. People of any age who believe what the Church teaches can be baptised. Usually parents choose to bring their babies for Baptism so that they belong to the Church community from an early age.

Babies are too young to speak for themselves, so their parents and godparents speak for them when they are baptised. The godparents promise to help the parents to bring the child up in the Christian faith.

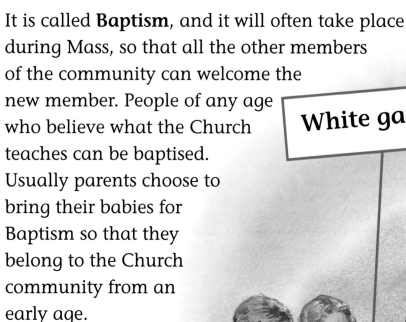

White garment

Water

Oil of Chrism

Candle

The baby is not able to choose for himself or herself whether they wish to be baptised, but the parents want their son or daughter to be a member of the Church community so that they are brought up to know about God's goodness.

There are many different signs used in Baptism, including:

Water: this is a sign of new life. When it is poured over the baby in Baptism it is a sign that the baby is sharing in the new life of Jesus.

Candle: Jesus is the Light of the World and the baptismal candle is a sign that the light of Jesus has entered the baby's life.

Oil of Chrism: a special oil that has been blessed by the Bishop is poured onto the baby's head as a sign of the presence of the Holy Spirit who will help the baby in his or her Christian life.

White garment: this is sometimes a white shawl. It is put on the baby as a sign that the baby has 'put on' Jesus and shares in the new life of Jesus.

Activities

1. Draw a candle and decorate it so that it will be a reminder that we are supposed to show God's love to others.

2. Imagine you are the photographer at a Baptism.

   (a) Which key moments would you want to photograph?

   (b) Explain why these moments are important.

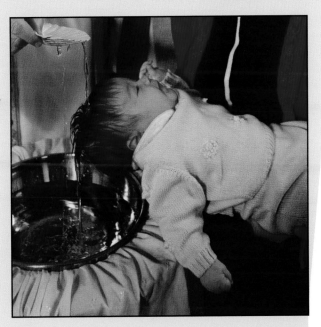

Word Box
godparent

What we believe

During Baptism, the child's family and friends say what they believe as Christians. This is something that happens at Mass as well. It is called the creed, from a Latin word, *credo*, meaning 'I believe'. It contains some very important statements, because to belong to the community of the Church, all the members need to agree that this is what they believe.

> "This is our faith. This is the faith of the Church.
> We are proud to profess it, in Christ Jesus, our Lord."
>
> (From the Service of Baptism)

Christians believe

- God is our Father. He is totally powerful and eternal.

- God created everything.

- Jesus is the Son of God.

- Jesus was born, lived and died to save us from sin and death.

- Jesus rose from the dead and ascended into heaven.

- Jesus will come again.

- The Holy Spirit is active in the world and in the Church today.

- We have the promise of God's mercy and of eternal life.

- We are part of the Communion of Saints.

The Communion of Saints *is* the Church - that is all the people who belong to the Church.

We are members of the 'Communion of Saints' - the Church community - we are united with all Christians, past, present and future.

The Communion of Saints

Remember that 'community' means that:

- Its members all share something in common.

- Being in a community can mean lots of good things - joys.

- But it also means challenges - things that we have to do to be good members of this community.

- There are rules that help the members to make a good community.

- Its members have a common purpose or beliefs.

- Some communities have special events.

- Different people have different roles within a community.

Activities

1. Read again the section on what Christians believe on page 84.

   (a) Draw an outline of Jesus' face.

   (b) Choose three sentences about Jesus, write them near his face and draw arrows to them.

   (c) Say why these sentences are important to you.

2. Imagine some inspectors are visiting the school.

   They know it is a Catholic school and they want to find out from the pupils what Catholics believe.

To help them to understand, write down:

   (a) what you think Catholics believe about Jesus;

   (b) what it means to belong to the community of the Church.

3. Is your school or church named after a saint?

   Try to find out about this saint and write a short story about him or her.

Word Box

Creed   Latin

85

The Church celebrates

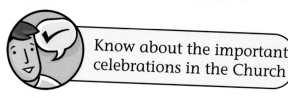

Have you ever celebrated your birthday with a party or been to a wedding or christening celebration?

We all enjoy a good celebration and fortunately there are so many things we can celebrate, like birthdays, baptisms, weddings, passing a test or an exam or hearing good news of any kind!

There are lots of different ways to celebrate too - getting together with friends, having a party, going out for a meal, sending cards or gifts.

Over a whole year the Church celebrates all the great events that show God's love for us.

We celebrate the birth of Jesus, his life and his teaching, his death and his resurrection.

We celebrate the lives of Saints and of Mary our Mother on their special feast days during the year.

One very important day the Church celebrates is the **Lord's day**. The Lord's day is every Sunday of every week. On this important day we celebrate Mass and remember Jesus' life, death and resurrection and his great love for each one of us.

The Church's seasons

Just as there are four seasons in the year - Autumn, Winter, Spring and Summer - so the Church year has seasons too!

In the Church's year there are **five** seasons: Advent, Christmas, Lent, Easter and Ordinary Time. Each season has its own colour.

On this page you can see a calendar of the seasons the Church celebrates during the year. Each year begins with Advent.

When the priest leads a celebration, he wears clothes called vestments. These are usually the same colour as the season, so during the season of Lent he will wear purple vestments and in Ordinary Time he will wear green.

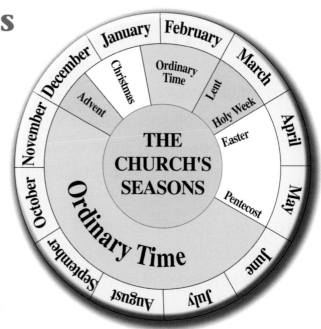

Advent and **Lent** are purple, a colour which shows that these are special times of waiting, preparation, and even penance.

Christmas and **Easter** are white, a colour which shows that we are celebrating very joyful events in the life of Jesus.

Ordinary Time is green; this is a time when we can grow closer to God through the ordinary, everyday things that we do because God is present in our lives all the time, as well as during special moments.

Activities

1. **(a)** Think about a birthday celebration that you really enjoyed - it may have been your own birthday or that of a friend.

   (b) Write or draw about the celebration, showing how you celebrated and who was there.

   (c) What did you enjoy most about this celebration?

2. Think about one celebration in the Church's year that you have enjoyed - perhaps a Christmas or a school Mass.

   (a) Write or draw about this celebration, showing what was being celebrated and who was there.

   (b) What did you enjoy about this celebration?

3. Here is a list of the five seasons of the Church. They are all jumbled up. Can you put them in the right order and match them up with a sentence to explain why they are important?

   Christmas

   Advent   Ordinary Time

   Easter   Lent

   A time to celebrate the birth of Jesus

   A time to celebrate the presence of Jesus in our ordinary lives

   A time to celebrate that Jesus rose from the dead

   A time to prepare for Christmas

   A time to prepare for Easter

4. See if you can find out during which season we celebrate the following feast days in the Church year:

   Epiphany   All Saints Day   Pentecost Sunday

   Write a few sentences about what the Church celebrates on each of these feasts.

Glossary

Abide - Stay, remain

Angel - A messenger from God

Anxiety - Worrying a lot about things

Apostle - The twelve closest
followers of Jesus

Ark - The place where the Ten
Commandments were kept.
It was the most Holy place for
the Jews

Arrested - Taken away and kept by
soldiers or police

Ascended - To rise up

Ascension - When Jesus went back
up to heaven

Authority - Power

Baptise - To give the Sacrament
of Baptism

Beliefs - What we know is true
about God

Betrayed - When a trusted person
lets you down

Bishop - A priest who is the leader of
a diocese

Blessings - Good things that come
from God

Calvary - The hill outside Jerusalem
where Jesus was crucified

Challenge - Something which is
difficult to do

Chosen one - The person who God
promised would save his people

Church - All the people who believe
in the Catholic Faith

Commands - Things that God wants
us to do

Commandments - These are also called 'words of life', instructions which God gave to us

Commit sin - To do something that we know is wrong and hurtful

Community - A group of people who gather together for a purpose

Conceived - The moment when a life begins

Contrition - Feeling sorry

Covenant - A very serious promise

Create - To make something from nothing

Creation - The time when God created the universe, the world, animals, plants and people

Creed - From the Latin word *credo* which means 'I believe'. It is an important list of the things Catholics believe

Criminal - Somebody who does things that are against the law

Descendants - Those in your family who come after you, your children, grandchildren etc.

Diocese - An area with lots of parishes with a bishop to look after them

Disciples - The people who follow and listen to Jesus

Disobedience - Not doing what you are told

Easter Sunday - The day when Jesus rose from the dead

Engaged - When two people promise that they will marry each other

Epiphany - When the three wise men see the baby Jesus

Eternal life - A life with God that never ends

Eucharist - another word for the Mass, it comes from a Greek word which means giving thanks

Executed - When somebody is put to death

False Gods - Things that take the place of God in our lives, like money

Foster father - A man who looks after a child instead of his real father

Galilee - The area around the Sea of Galilee where Jesus lived and taught

Garden of Gethsemane - A Garden outside Jerusalem also known as the Mount of Olives where Jesus liked to pray

Glory - The praise or credit given for something that has been done well

Godparent - Someone who promises to help bring a baptised person up as a Christian

Good News - The meaning of the word Gospel

Graces - A help or gift which comes from God

Greeting - The first thing that is said when two people meet, like 'Hello' or at the annunciation, 'Hail, Mary'

Guardian - Somebody who looks after a child in the place of its parents

Guilty - To be responsible for something wrong that has happened

Handmaid - A servant, ready to do whatever God wants

Holy Trinity - The three persons, God the Father, God the Son and God the Holy Spirit who are three persons in one God

Holy Week - The seven days from Palm Sunday to Easter Sunday

Jewish - The Religion which began with Abraham and to which Jesus belonged

Judas - The disciple who betrayed Jesus

Justice - Fairness

Lamb of God - A name given to Jesus because he was sacrificed for our sins

Last Supper - Jesus' last Passover meal with his disciples when he gave them the Sacrament of Eucharist for the first time

Latin - The language spoken by the Romans and still the official language of the Catholic Church

Laws - Important rules

Martyr - Somebody who dies or suffers for what they believe

Mass - The Sacrament of the Eucharist

Messiah - The person who God promised would save his people

Mission - Teaching or preaching the word of God

Nazareth - The town where Joseph, Mary and Jesus lived

New Testament - The twenty-seven books of the Bible including the gospels that begin with the birth of Jesus and tell the story of how the Church began

Nineveh - The oldest and greatest city in the world

Offering - To give

Old Testament - The forty-six books of the Bible which tell the story from creation until before the birth of Jesus

Paradise - Heaven

Parishes - The area Catholics live in where they have their Church and a priest to look after them

Passover meal - The special meal that Jews have to remember their escape from Egypt

Pentecost - The day when the Holy Spirit came down on the apostles

Persecute - Hurting people because of what they believe

Philistines - A warlike people who lived near Israel

Pope - The person who takes the place of St Peter as leader of the Church

Presented - All first-born Jewish males were brought to God at the temple in Jerusalem to show that they belonged to Him

Priest - A man called to serve God's people in a special way, who has received the Sacrament of Ordination

Prophets - A holy person in the Bible, who hears God's word and tells others about it

Rabbi - A teacher of the Jewish faith

Reconciliation - The sacrament we receive when we confess and receive forgiveness for our sins

Religion - Belief in the existence of a superhuman power

Repented - sorry for their sins and made up for them

Resurrection - When Jesus rose from the dead on Easter Sunday

Revolution - A sudden and very big change

Roman governor - The person sent by the Roman Emperor to control a part of the empire

Romans - The most powerful people in the world when Jesus was alive

Sacrament - A very important gift from Jesus when we receive special help and grace

Sacrifice - To give something to God

Salvation - To be saved by God from sin and death

Scrolls - Long sheets of rolled up paper or parchment where the word of God was written

Sea of Galilee - A large lake in the area where Jesus lived

Self-control - Not to let the urge to do bad things control you

Service - A religious meeting where the Word of God is read

Shema - A word in the Jewish language which means Listen, it is also the name given to the list of the most important beliefs of the Jews

St Peter's - The large Church in Rome where St Peter is buried

Synagogue - Place where Jews gather together to read the word of God

Temple - The special place where God was worshipped in Jerusalem

Tomb - A place where someone is buried

Torah - The first five books of the Old Testament

Vestments - The special clothes that a priest wears at Mass

Warrior - A soldier or fighter

Witnesses - People who have been with Jesus and tell others about him

Word of God - The Bible, collected over many centuries by the Jewish people and the Church

Worship - To adore, respect, praise

Writing tablet - What was used in Roman times instead of writing paper

Nihil obstat: Father Anton Cowan (Censor).
Imprimatur: The Very Rev Alan Hopes, VG, Westminster, 29 June 2002, Feast of Ss Peter & Paul

© 2002 The Incorporated Catholic Truth Society
Published 2002 by The Incorporated Catholic Truth Society,
40-46 Harleyford Road,
London SE1 5AY
Tel: 020 7640 0042   Fax: 020 7640 0046
website: www.cts-online.org.uk

ISBN: 1 86082 166 9   CTS Code: Pr 04
Designed and Produced by: The Catholic Truth Society/Stephen Campbell.
Picture research: The Catholic Truth Society/Pierpaolo Finaldi.
Front cover: Jesus the Teacher © Adrian Barclay/ Beehive Illustration.
Printed by: Arkle Print Limited.

Acknowledgments
Considerable thanks are due to the teachers in the following schools who contributed to the development of this Pupil Book 4 by way of advice, editorial review and comment. The Way, the Truth and the Life Series has been a collaborative exercise: kind thanks are expressed in particular to the following schools: Farleigh School, Andover; Notre Dame School, Greenwich; Our Lady of Lourdes School, Barnet; Sacred Heart School, Barnet; St Teresa's School, Harrow; St Agnes' School, Barnet; St Vincent's School, Barnet; St Raphael's School, Ealing.

Editorial Team
Anne Marie Alison, Louise McKenna, Amette Ley, Elizabeth Redmond, Anthony O'Rourke, Laura Lamb, Fergal Martin, Miriam and Marcellina Cooney.

Professional Curriculum Adviser   **Theological Adviser**
Margaret Cooling   Mgr Michael Keegan

Illustrations: © Philip Hood / Arena. © Adrian Barclay, © Darrell Warner/ Beehive Illustration; © Gilly Marklew/ S.G.A. © Kevin Maddison/ Allied Artists Ltd; © Peter Dennis/ Linda Rogers Associates.

Permission credits: Photography on pages 5,49,56,74,75,81,83,86,87 © Lorenzo Lees. Page 21: St Francis Receiving the Stigmata by El Greco (1541-1614) Private Collection, Madrid, Spain/Bridgeman Art Library; St Therese of Lisieux at the age of 15 in April 1888. Page 23: St John the Baptist by Titian (c. 1488-1576) Galleria dell'Accademia, Venice, Italy/Bridgeman Art Library. Page 29: The Flight into Egypt by Juan Leon Gerome (1824-1904) Whitford & Hughes, London, UK/Bridgeman Art Library. Page 31: The Adoration of the Shepherds by Domenichino, courtesy of the National Galleries of Scotland. Page 39: © Peter Turnley/CORBIS, © Howard Davies/CORBIS, © Steve Raymer/CORBIS. Page 47: The Raising of Jairus' daughter by Edwin Longsden Long (1829-1911) Victoria Art Gallery/Bridgeman Art Library. Page 56: © Carlos Reyes Manzo/Andes Press Agency, Christ before Caiaphas by Niccolo Frangipane (fl. 1563-1597), Galleria e Museo Estense, Modena, Italy/Bridgeman Art Library. Page 66: The Ascension of Our Lord, Russian icon from the Malo-Kirillov Monastery, Novgorod School, 1543 Museum of Art Novgorod, Russia/Bridgeman Art Library. Page 68: St Peter Preaching in Jerusalem (fresco) by Tommaso Masolino Brancacci Chapel, Santa Maria del Carmine, Florence, Italy/Bridgeman Art Library. Page 72: The Conversion of St Paul by Michelangelo Merisi da Caravaggio (1571-1610) Santa Maria del Popolo, Rome, Italy/Bridgeman Art Library. Page 76: © Mug Shots/CORBIS, © Julian Hirshowitz/CORBIS; poem reprinted by permission of PFD on behalf of Roger McGough © Roger McGough: as printed in the original volume. Page 81: © Danny Lehman/CORBIS, © Michael Lewis/CORBIS. Page 84: Fol. 151v The Last Judgement, Italian School (16th century) Biblioteca Reale, Turin, Italy/Bridgeman Art Library.